WITA WITALANA

By the same author:

Nightmares Run Like Mercury
Dancing Home

WITA WITALANA

(look out over)

PAUL COLLIS

RECENT WORK PRESS
2015-2025
10 YEARS OF POETRY

Wita Witalana
Recent Work Press
Canberra, Australia

Copyright ©Paul Collis 2025

ISBN: 9781763670174 (paperback)

A catalogue record for this book is available from the National Library of Australia

All rights reserved. This book is copyright. Except for private study, research, criticism or reviews as permitted under the Copyright Act, no part of this book may be reproduced, stored in a retrieval system, or transmitted in any form by any means without prior written permission. Enquiries should be addressed to the publisher.

Cover image: Ron Lech via pexels
Cover design: Recent Work Press
Set by Recent Work Press

recentworkpress.com
10 YEARS OF POETRY

With all love,
Wita Witalana *is dedicated to my mother, Valma Dawn, who could not read, but continued to buy me books throughout my primary school years, and so, did encourage me to learn and to read.*

And, **Wita Witalana** *is also dedicated to my Uncle, John (Fight) Knight and my wonderful Cousin (The Ghost), Alan Knight, AKA, Oscar the Grouch. Thanks for looking out for me, JK and Oscar, and for now looking over me from above.*

Contents

Foreword by Samuel Wagan Watson   ix

ONE

On The Hop	3
So Deep the Blue ...	4
Home	5
Yellow Day	8
Quiet, Yellow Morning	9
Little Ghost	10
Deep Water	11
Situation in Sydney ...	12
Blood Hearts	13
Skin	14
Ghost Steps	15
Scatter Little Children	16
Sleepin-in Drinkin	17
Blood Brothers	18
Moonlit Stray	19
Burning Star	21
There I Am	22
Wita Witalana (look out over)	23

TWO

Return	27
Sacred Place	28
Marrawa	29
Brown Snake Night ... Sing to Me Too	31
Speaking of Violence on Women's Country	33
Woman's Country	35
Fantasies	44
Strangers in That Country	46

Nemarluk Country	48
Wananmpi Tjukurpa	56
Belfast Spring	57
Healing the Wounded	58
About Last Night	59
Full Moon Dreaming On Kamilaroi Country	60
Carrying Hearts	62

THREE

Shady	65
The Belonging Man	67
They Came Together	70
Spooky!	71
re[her]sal	74
Some Popular Australian Mistakes (22 Thoughts on a Dead Bullock)	75
I See You	78
Tomorrow	80
Reconcile That	81
Through My Window	84
Through Your Window	85
Through Our Window	86
Tomorrow Tonight	87
Sometimes	88
Guys Like Me They Don't Want	89

Foreword

It is once again a pleasure to welcome a new birthing unto the world from Dr Paul Collis with a fresh and premium selection of verse and prose poetry. Congratulations to Recent Work Press for championing Collis a second time. WITA WITALANA builds upon this visionary's opus, NIGHTMARES RUN LIKE MERCURY and his David Unaipon award-winning, 'KOORI-NOIR', fictional debut, DANCING HOME with University of Queensland Press. The searing 'Barkindji' voice reminds us that so much remains unreconciled in the depravity of colonialism, crimson brush strokes on tarnished Dreaming. Paul's writing coruscates with grass-root poetic flourishes. We are also gifted with illustrations of his romantic longing in 'Belfast Song' and blessed by Collis' collaborative techniques with other poets and academics. For enthusiasts of his past work each new page contains an *objet d'art* in rare and poignant, textual significance...WITA WITALANA—LOOK OUT OVER—for where this poet-warrior's passionate battle cry can reach!

Samuel Wagan Watson, Brisbane, 2025

ONE

On The Hop

Dependin' on your Ride,
it takes 21 minutes from Mascot to The Cross
Dependin' how much you're hangin' out,
it takes 10 minutes to get to Pete's Place from Mascot
Dependin' on how much Johnny Cash you have,
it takes 5 minutes from Glenn's old place to the Shops
Dependin' on the number of them Blue Shirts,
It only takes 8 big steps to the back fence if you're On The Hop.

So Deep the Blue …

I thought I would die.
Before …
I reached 19.
Somehow. I thought my death would be.
Silent. Violent.
But death passed me, somehow.
The Dart swerved and missed me.
Somehow, the shadow passed over.
Took my friend George.
I cried, when he died.
Didn't go to his funeral.
Instead, Death became a companion.
Regular. Permanent. Consistent.
And, then I turned 30.
When Death took my great strength, my Grandfather died.
I died too.
A little.
I stopped the car. Ice wind swept through me, and I knew he died.
The sky went
Dark … like blood.

Home

Archie was born at Gundabooka, sometime in the early 1900's.

Archie was a Barkindji person. Archie's mother's name was Lisa.

Archie's father was Hero.

Gundabooka is the big Corroboree Ground.

But Parks and Wildlife own that Country now ... no more dances there now ... no more Ceremonies.

It was a place where Barkindji, Nyempa, Murrawarri, Wonkamarra, Bonkamarra, Kamilaroi, Wailwan, Wiradjuri all came to practise Law, to Corroboree, and to share culture.

Gundabooka is on Barkindji country, and it is shared with Nyempa people.

Gundabooka is where the cave paintings are.

Gundabooka had permanent sweet water, once, that sprung from a spring in the ground.

Gundabooka was Archie's Home.

When Gundabooka was taken from the Barkindji people by white people, Archie went and lived in Bourke. 'I'll never go back 'ome— not again. White fella now. All that country.'

Archie came to Bourke, lived in a caravan, alone, over on the flood plain, on the other side of the railway line.

Archie lived there, near the cemetery, among blue gum trees, out of view from the town.

'You like livin' here?' I asked him.

'Ahh … it's better than nowhere, I s'pose,' Archie answered.

'You like it back there? Gundabooka?' I asked him.

He smiled. 'Yeah. Good there. Everything was good there' he said.

'I love you Grandfather. I'm sorry you don't have Home anymore,' I said.

'Love you too, Grandson,' he replied.

I was borne in Bourke in the late 1950s.

My father was Thomas. He was a Wailwan person. A fighter.

My mother was Valma. Valma's mother was Ruby. Ruby was a Kunya Law Woman.

Ruby married Archie.

Valma and Thomas were both born on Nyempa country, in the place of tall trees—Brewarrina.

Valma and Thomas were born without a Home. They were born on Mission ground.

Valma and Thomas met and fell in love.

They were married and lived in Bourke. They lived on the Reserve at first, and later, after the flood, they moved into the town of Bourke.

'You like livin' here, Dad?' I asked Thomas.

Thomas screwed his face into a snarl, 'Too many bloody Police, for me, boy,' he said.

'Me too,' I said.

'Mum, you like it here?' I asked Valma.

'Ahh … it's alright. Better than nowhere, I s'pose,' Valma said.

Bourke was Barkindji country once.

White people took that land from Barkindji people with guns and soldiers and keep it under Australian law.

Sometimes, I'd go over the railway line, and sleep on the ground.

I'd lay under the gum trees near Grandfather's caravan.

We'd talk late into the night.

He would tell me about the sweet water at Gundabooka.

He would tell me about fishing trips and 'good Country'.

And he spoke about his brothers, who went to the big War (WW1).

He spoke about his brother who didn't return from that war.

He told how his brother died from gas poisoning when he was fighting other men, in France.

And he spoke about his other brother, the war hero, Albert, who came back. He spoke about how Albert lived alone, way out on the flood plain with no country, in a tin hut that he'd built from the kerosene tins he collected from the rubbish tip.

And Grandfather spoke of his 'little Brother', Bill, who returned from that first world war, minus his left arm.

'I love you Grandfather,' I said.

'Love you too, Grandson,' he replied, and then I would fall asleep.

Back to Country.

Yellow Day

Blue.
Hot face, turning down.
The road turns bitumen to dust.
We all arrive.
Waku's do the talking
with low and loud callings
as if to say, He's here now.
And with the priest's final prayer,
they lay Grandfather down.
Back to Country.

Quiet, Yellow Morning

She was buried yesterday. In the cemetery, they laid her down.
Forever time.
Been mostly raining up there.
She was killed.
Rain washes her tracks from the earth, making it a re-birth.
Tears and pain.
Killing is no loving game.
I called cousins, afterwards—
Kev and Trev, the pall bearers, said it was the quietest wake ever.
I sat in Cook. Drank myself to sleep.
Don't know what time it was, but it was late when I rested.

The sun rose.
Quiet, yellow morning.

Out the back, dressed in the black I'd slept in,
I sat, listened to birds' chirp.
The sun warmed me. I whispered, 'Goodbye'.
I'm okay.
I'll be right again.
I'll, I'll write again.
I'll talk to someone.
I'll Play ABBA songs, (her favourite band).
She could really sing well. I Do, I Do, I Do, was her favourite.
I can't stop my leg from shaking …
Shaking like a hungry junkie, I am.
Hung out.
I'll be okay, it's just that the shock, ringing loud,
you know … hitting me hard.

Little Ghost

I walked, old footsteps
around the street
where Harriett walked.

I walked in yellow sunlight
where She walked, The Ghost Girl.

On darkest night, without sound, Harriett walks the street
dressed in white.
Slow and alone.

I follow her footsteps.
The sun was warm
when I walked where Harriett trod.
I was bathed in yellow light, and warm.
But you don't see me, Harriett.
Can you hear me, Harriett?

Others have seen You. On that road.
They watch you stop at the corner.
Oh Harriett, who are you waiting for?

You have been there for so long …
Slowly. Alone.
I follow your footsteps …
bathed in yellow light, not seeing you.

Deep Water

Teneale,
that's your name, hey.
Yeah ... Teneale.
Good name, too.
Strong name, that one ...
like that Obi-Wan Kenobi, from Star Wars.
Strong name.
I knew you were strong
at the Majik Lake, when I met you,
that day.
There was a distance in your eyes ...
I seen it.
Strength behind your smile, I thought.
You are a writer of a different kind.
You, and the Majik Lake, got history ...
Both deep water
you two.

Situation in Sydney...

'Na. Not doin' that. Not goin' to rehab'.
And then, there's that silence. You know?
Denial everywhere.
Denial in silence.
(Her skinny little body, a tremble. Her eyes fill with shame and pain.)
I search her face for a sign, just one little memory, of her.
She knows what I'm looking for.
Eye's overflow. 'I'm sorry, Uncle'.

I remember Christmas morns in PJs,
and her, lost beneath a mountain of wrapping papers.
Laughter with smiley faces.
Tears of joy as seven bells rang out loud.
Everywhere the Christmas bells.

First day at school in brand new uniform,
slowly turn to
first cigarettes and boyfriend kisses.
Movie dates and birthday cakes,
she quietly slipped away into a grown-up world.
For a moment though, she's back—that shiny-faced little kid,
back with me,
for a second.

I searched the city for a bed in a Rehab.
But all the beds were taken.
All the doors turned closed.

Despair. Now everywhere despair.
Everywhere ...

Blood Hearts

She
had a name
was educated
Her education taught—
how to duck,
to stand-up and take it laying down
She
    grew like that
She
understood music—
the bang-bang kind of country
              a simple melody
with a hard punch line …

He remembered nothing … 'Bad dream—Jest bad dreamin'.'
When the deed was done
he sat alone
        shock setting-in
he waited, quiet
            Cops took him in
removed from the scene
the lights went down
but the violence surrounds
Her memory drowned
Destroyed children
witness to the night.

Skin

Hello Brother, I say
from within the Skin—
the Skin of my Mother
the Skin of Kunya.
Hello Brother, I repeat—
from the Skin of Ancestors
that Skin, from when Time
had no counting.
Hello again Brother, I offer the Wind
that came from the Plains.
That Wind, it is Forever.
That Wind, that was the Only Breath
to All Skin,
that began when there was no Time counting.

Ghost Steps

Thinking Country, to memories …
splashing around with evening hush …
imagining Country without Dreaming …
Is it nowhere land?
Who are those Ghost shadows
who leave no footprint?
Wind howls, a swirl.
Hush. Hush.
Wind is telling story.

Scatter Little Children

While Rome burns candles,
I dreamed a Ghost wind that carried ghost voices.
Some dreaming stayed inside,
a moment's rest.

Ideas broke open and Covid reigned.
The Virus hit Barkindji Dreamers in Bourke as Ghost Dreaming.
In fear and un-knowing,
new kings, wore masks, hovering over the dying.

Scatter, little children and old people.
Hide to keep safe.
Dreaming, Dreaming, screaming Dreaming.

Some cannot stand the Dreaming
Old people dreamed while blood clotting.
Children coughed up ghost stories.

My little children and old people
dreamed into the dark.
Dreams lay scattered in the ghost wind.

Sleepin-in Drinkin

I've slept with the old moll, many times.
I've woken up with her,
all over my skin,
and deep within.
She caressed me, looked bright at night,
and brought the stars into my light,
and made my world go dark, again.

Blood Brothers

I cough blood these days—
from working without masks
breathin' in the dust.
The fumes burned my nose and made it bleed,
and burned my throat.
I could see the waves of poison rise from the work
like heat wave apparitions.
My uncle died from the fumes—with
an unknown cancer, the doctor said.
I'm fucked, my uncle said.
Softly.
He reached for me that last time
in hospital.
His life sweated out of him.

I cough blood these days.
I'm fucked.

Moonlit Stray

Meow
Meow
Me *oh*.
And, accompanied with a scratching on the wire around my window,
faint sound reached me …
wide eyes peered through the pane …

Meow. Meow.
Connie, that you?

The window detached, and in crawled Connie, the girl I knew.
She looked like a wild little stray in that moonlit hour.
Oh Connie … Connie. Good to see you.

Connie crawled into my arms, whispered, Hungry, I'm Hungry …
Connie ate my chocolate biscuits and drank the day-old milk.

Connie, what's wrong? Connie where have you been?
I'm on the run. Runnin' away. Runnin'. Runnin'. Runnin' free, to you.

Whiskey and milk sunk Connie down,
into my pillow she slept. Oh Connie, where have you been?
You shine, and sneak into my room in a moonlit hour, my lovely.
Will you stay?

I sleep too, holding tight, my lovely Connie,
into dark hours, I slept with her …
in the morning, Connie paced the floor, scratching at the door …

She wanted to run again.
To be Runnin'. Runnin'. Runnin'
to be free from me one last time.

Burning Star

I wonder if you're sleeping
and where do you go
when tiredness is tedium
and you seem alone.
A distance. A dance,
a place that's your own …

Last night I watched a star
burn the night sky.
I saw the trail of tears behind Her.
She burned right away.
And I wondered if you're sleeping.

There I Am

For me, sleep has a cost.
A cost I pay, when sleep does come.
I don't pay a Ferry man.
I don't pay no Guide.
There's no one there
That takes me by the hand …
I go
And there I am.
In the place where there's no sound.
Where everything is everyone.
But I'm not one with them.
They know me …
No.
I know them …
But nobody makes a sound.
Their lips move. Eyes flash a look.
Then they face each other. Again.
Locked in a gaze.
I walk.
On, and alone.
Each step, silent.
There is no breath.
No doorway.
No light.
No footprint.
There is no ground.

Wita Witalana (look out over)

At the tree, he sat, spoke wise
through the wind, hear the message,
the tree is signpost.
Be quiet.
Be still.
Hear the message:

Wita Witalana ... Wita Witalana
        (looking out over)
they come, they come
        Wita Witalana—
Steel Wom-boo.

Axe sounds rang across my Mother's
belly ...
Watchtower's fields of love lay slain.
        no more boomerang from
trees
        no more spears
        no more Mother's
signpost.
You left axe marks on my Mother,
Wom-boo,
—through sacred totem—you cut my
heart.
Rainbow Serpent's tears cannot
make the slain grow again.

In towns

it rains, cold
so cold I ache ...
because I'm alone,
away from you—

no more boomerang from trees—
no more spears ...

TWO

Return

Returning ... to Earth. To Mother.
I expect my inheritance.
And my soul embraced,
By another body—
Might be:
Rock,
Cloud,
Light,
Scent,
Person,
Plant,
Animal,
Wind,
Water ...

Barkindji.

Sacred Place

People call you Darling, but
I say Barka.

Sometimes you look sick—
A lime green, you turn ... Sometimes, blue.
Sometimes, you're a milky/yellow.

You're never clean ... Anymore.

My old people spoke about you. Telling
that you were clean and clear. Once.

Fish could see the Sun from 20 metres
beneath your surface.

You smell rotten. Now.
The smell of decay and clay.

I hear the wind blow through the Red Gums
as it comes around the Bend. And near the Weir.
One can taste the mud in your waters.

You have been poisoned with fertilizers
and waste.

You were made by Rainbow Serpent
and to be Sacred.

Marrawa

Oxide Blood Work

Heat waves drifting on canvas

And fingerprints are everywhere

Over country.

Mesmerizing. Blinding.

But eyes can't stare away.

Taken deeper, deeper into Oxide Blood.

Into the essence of purpose and desire.

Then, there's the face—eyes first

That Country in …

And everything, in that Country.

How many times,

Be long Country?

How many times,

Be come Country?

The stream of life runs in you.

It flows across the Canvas. And

Again, your fingerprint and essence of purpose appears

Beneath the surface.
Spirits. Totems. Ancient watercourse. Burials

Change again.
Ghost Bird. Wings stretched wide, not facing,
But flying away.

The desert heat lays in the Red Earth—the Oxide with the fire fury

Imagine the burning …
The Whiteman there with the straight nose, appears
Painted large and obvious … But had to look to see him.

Small eye on the prize—Country.

Brown Snake Night ... Sing to Me Too

It was a Brown Snake night,
last night yellow moon
filled in sorry news—
the passing of an elder language teacher.

Ngai old man. Ngai.
I speak in Barkindji ...
in Kunya,
in Wonkamarra,
in Muruwari,
and in Nyemba.

When we lose good language speakers
purlu-karntu, purlu-karntu
our language lays dying in a dark past.
We're threatened.
Without language
how can we speak?

Now we are out of turn
purlu-karntu, purlu-karntu
broken,
messed up.

Ahh ...
sing me then...
make me wom-boo
turn me to ghost.
Let me see old people, again.

Let me see wizened faces,
touch hands, again,
let me walk with them.

I long for campfire talk,
to hear Murrdie language spoken in the bush, teaching
at night in the Milky Dust.
See the shiny lights of mica-ochre,
glint,
on the Brown Snake moon-dancer bodies.

Let the stories
be expressed, dance
on powdery ground
and …
Sing me, too
Sing me too.

Speaking of Violence on Women's Country

The town of Bourke, in far north-western New South Wales, is unceded Barkindji Country, and home to 27 language groups. Bourke became a centre for Western pastoral and agricultural industry following white colonial settlement in the 1830s. By the late 20th century, the once-booming wool industry had been superseded by cotton, with cotton one face of an underlying and cut-throat harvesting and trade in water. From early in the colonial period, traditional and totemic trees in this area, as elsewhere in Australia, were massacred, and ceremonial sites destroyed in an effort to rid the land of evidence of Aboriginal ownership and Aboriginal ways. Human massacres also took place, usually unprosecuted and often still unacknowledged. Legal fiction abounds. The white poet, Henry Lawson, who lived in Bourke for some time, famously wrote that 'if you know Bourke, you know Australia,' but much of Aboriginal experience remains unseen and unremembered by white Australia.

Barkindji Country is Women's Dreaming, which means Women's Law—the law of matriarchy, which both women and men help to carry out. Barkindji Country is the resting place of Mungo Lady, who was cremated some 42,000 years ago, to emerge again in 1968. Country holds the bones and stories of ancestors, and at times returns them to us.

We wrote the poem 'Woman's Country' during a recent research visit to Bourke, during a rare period of flood. Much of the previous 25 years (particularly 1997-2009 and 2017-2019) had been marked by dire and ongoing drought, exacerbated by industrial water theft and overuse, alongside climate change. Among the consequences are great strain and grief for Aboriginal communities as they see their rivers, here the Barka (the Darling), emptying, threatening the continuity of life, culture and Dreaming. When asked, 'What is a river?' in our research discussions, traditional owner Wayne Knight answered, 'That river is our spiritual lifeblood.' When the river was empty, Barkindji children asked, 'Where does the Rainbow Serpent sleep now?'

Although the return of a flood period replenishes Country, the exploitation of water continues, and the children's question continues to haunt Barkindji people's visions of the future. It is estimated that 20-30% of the current floodwaters are being diverted to industrial dams, often well beyond legal quotas. This water will never reach deep into Country to replenish trees, billabongs and rivers ahead of the next drought.

Bourke—on the edge of the desert—could be a hard place to live for those who came to take it, because of heat, water, weather and distance from Sydney, and because of colonial determination to rewrite the laws of Country. Racist violence and oppression have been a feature of white presence in the town since colonisation. Women's Law continues, but is continually threatened. Where cultural continuity is repressed and broken, more violence floods in. Although the town purportedly has one of the highest police-citizen ratios in Australia, methamphetamine ('ice'), alcohol and other drugs are readily available, often more so than services and resources to support individuals and the maintenance of cultural ways that protect and guide. Regardless, these ways continue.

Woman's Country

With Jen Crawford

W: Voice as a woman
M: Voice as a man
V: Voices
Also speaking are Whiteness, Blackness, Country, the Law

M   in Bourke,
       writing
       still on the road,
       out on the track
       windin' back on ghost wind
       touchin' spirits

       glimpses of family
       the living and others who have passed
       flash shadows
       bloodstains on cemented paths

       black earth country beneath my feet
       lookin' at Barka

       shadow places everywhere
       dark places where love found life
       shadow places where life found death
       things fade

       I walk where the old man walked
       on ceremonial ground

dancin' up dust
from day to night

•

near the courthouse,
trade
echoes float easy on night breeze
you're still on my mind

in shadows, blood boys
with eyes on desire

woman's law, this place
girls rush across
flashing eyes long enough
ask the unspeakable question
like little ghosts
they disappear into shadows

morning brings tired old voices
Barka grows wilder
stretching herself with new life.
Aunt takes to talk of night things
of being sung to the charm
of a clever man

•

W   you be a pedestrian light,
green: walk now
walk quick
don't run

    signalling
    from the door of the chemist
    your face as calm as a mother's

    I cross

    blood pilot
    calls behind me
    wings out at full stretch

    •

V   whisper
    Mooda-Gutta

    •

W   young men fly the streets
    blood pilots with cut faces
    turn me female
    turn me glue-footed
    back on myself

    •

V   I cross the road when I see them coming
    I check both sides of the street before I get out of the car
    I get back in the car when I get that feeling
    I lock the doors; wind up the windows

    •

W   although
    six kinds of bird are singing their songs
    and the breeze is gentle in the red river gums
    that run long fingers through the water's flow
    and the sunlight's strong

on the stricken and on me

•

V red-tailed black cockatoos cry welcome

women's country
river overflowing

•

W departure halls fill up with mobilized soldiers
and we go too, me and these men,
my friends, travelling companions,
into the mouth of our violence
carried on through each checkpoint
weaving back all the while

•

W suck the milk, they call
to each other
on the verandah, on the street
in the studio, in dreams
suck the milk!
suck the milk, they call to the sunset
to the inundated trees

& each
approaches the milk, enters the milk
laps, & sucks, &
breathes in the air
sweetness of night flowers
all of music, all philosophy

•

M   I was born to woman's country
       woman's dreaming
       woman's law
       creation stories.
       Women's Country.

       Embraced in women's dreaming
       we are held, raised up
       take our women's name, our mother's name,
       not our father's.
       aunties, too, become mothers to us.
       It's all a woman's embrace—
       plants, animals, water,
       life.
       All woman's country
       and woman's dreaming.

       •

V   rain comes, the ground is soaked
       floodwater rises
       earth slips
       not all bones are in the right place

       •

V   whisper
       Mooda-Gutta

       •

W   I'll be Country
       you be Country too

       I'm in the milk and the milk's in me

       •

W   night comes earlier and earlier

        there he is
        by the bowling club gate
        reeling in place, rolling a smoke
        bung eye, bleeding cheek

        will I slip past unseen
        ghost on black ice
        a chill

        •

M   some dance some night kardatchi man from out of town
        plucks one hair from her head. 'If I want you, you'll come.'

W   where else would she go but the police? trust
        held out in her hand. dragonfly.
        'Can you help me? He said he'd sing me.'
        Where would she have gone, but for the police?
        Rows of the silenced.
        Rows of protectors cut down.
        To the police: 'listen: he took my hair.'

        •

M   hunger
        sly things happen on the sly
        there is violence in threatening breaths,
        and young men with blood faces screaming into the night

        hungry, craving … nothing is not enough,
        everything is never enough,
        everywhere the hunger,
        and the law can go and hide like the slimy dog it is

it's never there when you need it, anyway.
Hide and slide, you dogs,
catch and kill your own out here,
the weak ones are targets and desired, the naive
try look tough, even while you're pissin' in your boots,
walk straight, walk fast, don't turn back to fight—
blood everywhere

•

M   I've touched that tree,
where she was.
Tears run with Barka
they are not different gamoo

•

M   woman's law, this place
filled and overflows on
Woman's Dreaming.
Country is a full belly
humming with life

•

W   little bug bangs the drum
crawls in me
can't get out
I'm reading my phone
on the floodplain at night
in the joyous proliferation

V   bang my head
bang a way in

W   standing at the door of the dark hospital
ringing the bell

me and these men, my friends

I'll be a jumping bean and you be two chairs
I'll be the dark and you be the eyes
I'll be here   when you hold my arm

W   but the bug will die in here
whole body kicking
against the drum

I'll be an orifice
I'll be a cell

•

V   I'll be here
dragonfly
floodplain in flood
one drop of rain
alive

•

V   stories, whispery voice
Mooda-Gutta!
warning sign, stampede horse.
Mooda-Gutta!
Waterspout ... sounds like petrol on fire—
don't cross there! *Mooda-Gutta*
don't say it

Notes on 'Woman's Country'

Barka: Barkindji name for the Darling River on Barkindji Country. Barka means 'my darling'.

Gamoo: water.

About *Mooda-Gutta* (or *Mundaguddah*), Kunya artist Brian Smith writes the following:
'I've heard it described as a serpent, sometimes even heard it connected to the rainbow serpent story, and it's definitely got connections up in Kunya country, where my family came from. But all the rivers around here, the Warrego, the Paroo, they all have clans and people that belong here, and they are all represented in Bourke, and they all have a story about the Mundaguddah. It may have different stories associated, but when you say that one word, it always means the same thing, "stay out of the water".

Those stories are important to our mob, and they kept us alive. In the simplest way, don't be near a dangerous place, like the river, without supervision. The sculpture [Andrew Hull's sculpture of Mundaguddah] has a gaping maw-like mouth and thousands of teeth like a cod, it could swallow you whole.'

Fantasies

Eyes lit up, wide
set on fire,
when they seen my country.

They struggled and lied
their way in.
Friended their way in,
said they were allies.
When that was not on
they fired the lead ...
and fired Mother earth, and hers ...

Oh, Oh, Country ...

White Fantasies ...
Black desired.

Country held her jewels,
underground.
White Imagination seen what was there ...
Green eyes, looking, looking ... Looking ...
friending their way in,
firing thundersticks.

Behind rocks and trees and from the grass,
Murrdie men came onto open Country,
and faced 'em on sandy ground.
Murrdie men stood, naked against them.
Spears flew from black hands

and lead and steel sunk black Warriors down …

And old Mother, accepted her children's blood.

Murrdie men fell together, in the thousands.
Back into Her arms.

Murrdie people fell quiet … We wait … Quiet.
And young warriors stagger the street, screaming at the Sky
while others do the big talk
with words, that fall like lead
with hearts that strike fire.

No one cares.

Essie told me, Murrdie people never say
truth of the heart,
not to allies.
Or those who benefit from theft.

Only bit a dirt we gonna git, if we lucky,
when we git six feet under, she spoke …
But some don't even git that dirt … they're thrown away into the furnace
or onto the river. No trace. No trace.

Oh. Oh …
Murrdie people.
Me people. Me people.

The Sun heats up
and Country burns an evening light …

Strangers in That Country

As true as Bakhtin said,
no word that you use has not been used before,
then, no footprint of yours, upon this land,
has not already been marked by black feet.

Claimed country by flag, you unknown bumbler,
you stumbled where my Grandfather had been,
to take by flag, a Country you do not know.
'Water. Where's water?' Lawson asked the black.
The black man smiled a discouraging disdain toward the author.
Black bony finger answered—to the West.
Lawson stumbled, found a dead cow, wrote *A Stranger on The Darling*.

Now you understand.
There is no place without a history.

That your wilderness was as cherished as cherry trees
by blacks.
That the calling to birds in early light
alerts where water is.
You slept in the wilds, and died by the dig tree,
unnecessarily.
You walked silently, craving with crusted blood tongues
in search and discovery, in earnest pride and adventure.
In time, you found your way across, beyond the dead cow,
and claimed the Darling your own.
Your discovery heralded across the land
in print.
A stranger no more, you Possessor.

Overturn the fragile soil with steel.
And with steel axe, take the trees away
and make fences to keep your own.
Still, you didn't see the ant tracks to the sweet stuff,
didn't hear the native bee's wings, nor did you understand.
In time, you drained your Darling, left her empty,
left her spread dead, then you ripped her from hip to hip …
and black hands broke bottles and strung rope

… then swung, at your disgust.

Nemarluk Country

There is no smoke or fire, it looks safe here to cross,
no rocks are out of place,
no footprints have been here.
Gee-up, horse.
And with a quiet slap of leather on hide,
they rolled on into the sacred river.

Cold water,
as clean as souls,
startled, stung, and refreshed
sweaty horses, and men.
No time for stopping, the new gods rode on through,
scooping drinks with their hats,
allowing just a couple of slurps for their beast.

Two men rode forward,
two stayed back …
for rearguard work, if needed.
They brandished side arms and long arms,
and a tame black,
who the new gods had forced to track.

And God made all
made everything
for new gods.
And the yellow metal, in the Daly River
was there
for the picking

but myalls had spoken just one name …
Nemarluk.
They warned, Nemarluk …
Nemarluk.
Shaking their worried heads to the new gods,
warning, that *He* was there.
Don't go to Nemarluk Country.

The new gods heard whispers of this wild one.
But, when questioned, tribal blacks kept lips tight.
Were they afraid of this Nemarluk too?
Or was it all superstition. All bullshit.

And God made all
made everything
for new gods. And the yellow metal,
in the Daly River,
was there
for the picking.

Apart from distant bush fires,
no smoke signals filled the air.
And birds had scattered.
The jingle of bridles
and the snorts from horses, filled the space with sound.
This silence, a new god thought, cannot be because of one man.
Only God can command such instance.
No black devil could quieten all birds, and lay down the bush …
So, on they pushed, deeper into Blackfella Country.

The tame man had not spotted marlu or other big game
for two days. Scared,

he looked for signs.
He skinned his eyes across the earth.
He peered into dark shadows.
And smelled the air for the scent of wild men.
He imagined that what wasn't there.
Becoming more afraid, he begged the new gods.
Go back. Go back. Too quiet—
Look …
Nothing there.
See.

And God made all,
made everything
for new gods.
And the yellow metal
in the Daly River
was there
for the picking.

One new god dreamed of the big mob.
Beef cattle king he'd be,
rich with the yellow gold.
Another god dreamed of the city,
new clothes, pocket watch, white woman.
The third god thought of good times,
all unto me, he thought.
The fourth god, being handsome,
thought of handsome things,
and everything dressed in yellow.

Go back. Go back, the tame man wished.

All he could find for food was snakes and goanna.
But with no appetite for food, he chewed on his thoughts.
And thought of his wife … about how she worried for him.
He thought of his fat son, of Marlu clan.
He thought of his father's country—of the high country,
where his father prayed.
And wished he had wings like Waku, the Crow.

Go back.
Go back, he wished.

Night came fast that evening.
The tame man smelled the air.
Too afraid to sleep, he listened to silence.
The air was hot and steamy.
He built the fire, bright … more wood. More wood.

The new gods smiled,
and kept their side arms cocked,
and the long arms filled with shot.
Tomorrow they would reap God's treasure
from the river.
The flies and mosquitoes, the bugs and winded horses,
soon, would be behind them.

The tame man trembled with worry.
He knew he would die first,
if spear or nulla-nulla flew from the bush.
He'd be first to go.
Sweat pooled beneath his eyes, in the cracks
and down his cheek.

Murrdie,
the tame man pointed towards the dark.

The new gods kneeled.
Back to back.
And faced the four winds
with side arms drawn.

Nemarluk and the Red Band of warriors
lay flat on the ground.
Only Mother Earth heard their heartbeats.
With killing spears beside them, Nemarluk
and the Red Band had come
to kill new gods.

The new gods held fast.
Full alert, their eyes searched for movement of the bush.
Their ears strained for sounds of attack.
And trigger fingers, itched for action.

And God made all
for new gods
and the yellow gold in the Daly River
was still there
for the picking.

On knees, the tame man's hands clutched Mother Earth.
He tried to control his breathing
but fear had him almost breathless.
He gulped air in big breaths
and for his efforts, received an elbow
from the first new god,

to his ribs,
to shut him quiet.

Nemarluk and the Red Band, waited
on. Into the night, they waited
for the new gods to give in to the silence.
Nemarluk waited for the new gods to tire.

God be with us.
God be for us.
God grant us victory,
the second new god prayed.

No moon showed her face that night.
After midnight, Nemarluk and the Red Band
disappeared from the scene. Back into the bush. They waited.

Yellow rays of golden sunlight streaked across the sky
when the tame man and the new gods rode out.
Saddlebags bulged with gold as they galloped away.

Nemarluk watched dust from the horses settle.
Nemarluk was in-Country, and
his Country was in him.
Nemarluk knew that there would be more new gods
coming for his Country now.
Coming, for the yellow gold,
in the Daly River, it was there
for the picking.

Notes for 'Nemarluk Country'

Nemarluk was born sometime in the late 1800's Northern Territory.

As a Warrior (Chief), Nemarluk had a small band of other warriors who all wore red head bands, giving rise the nick-name, the Red Band.

In the early 1900's Nemarluk let it be known to Aboriginal people throughout his tribal country that he would not stand for any white person to be on, or in the Daly River, searching for gold.

Two white men and an Aboriginal guide did however arrive at the Daly River to pan for gold.

On that occasion, Nemarluk and the Red Band of warriors lay in wait to kill the gold prospectors.

The Aboriginal guide was terrified, and though he could not detect any sign of Nemarluk of the Red Band, he alerted the white prospectors saying that he could 'smell wild men'. It is extremely doubtful that he would have smelled any scent of Nemarluk or the Red Band as those men had not washed and were the smell of Country.

The white men drew guns and kneeled back-to-back with loaded weapons, alert throughout the night hours. Nemarluk and the Red Band did not attack but withdrew from the scene without being seen or noticed. The white men and the Aboriginal guide were able to leave the area the next day without injury.

A short while after that incident, two more gold prospectors arrived and began panning for gold in the Daly River. On that occasion, Nemarluk and his warriors ambushed the prospectors at night and they were killed.

Nemarluk and his wife were both arrested and locked in the new prison that had been recently opened at Fanny Bay.

Neither Nemarluk or his wife had ever been inside a white person's building before that time. One can only imagine the horror that Nemarluk and his wife may have experienced inside the sandstone walls of the prisons.

Nemarluk was able to escape the jail and went on the run. Way up in the burial ground he camped. A 'black tracker' by the name of Bul-Bul was brought from Queensland to track Nemarluk.

One day, it was said that Nemarluk covered one hundred miles, on foot across sandy desert without leaving a track. He placed his toes beneath clumps of spinifex grass and moved from one clump to another, leaving no visible sign.

As good as Nemarluk was, he was eventually tracked by Bul-Bul, was arrested and placed back in Fanny Bay Prison. There would be no escape this time for Nemarluk.

Nemarluk died in that prison about three years later. Whether he was chained to a wall or to the floor, or flogged to death, or starved, we will never know the true cause of his death.

Nermarluk's people lamented that the Warrior Chief died from a broken heart.

Wananmpi Tjukurpa

(A painting by Tiger)

The paint looks like its peeling from the canvas,
but it's not peeling at all.
He has tricked my eyes with his style, that artist.
The camp sites, look like bomb craters ...
holding dots of family groups. Packed together. Tightly.

I fly my eyes to above the paint, to see old watercourses,
and tree-lined feet highways, wander through bends
around the four corners of his world.
It's a long river, that one. Like a snake, in the shaping
by the Rainbow Serpent.
Or is it, a Dreaming Track, those bends.
It is desert Country made of red rock and yellow sand.
It is big Country, that one.
As wide. As beauty.

Belfast Spring

It's so far out, and far away,
here.
Missing you ... I know I'm not meant to,
but I do.
Missing you
is the look on my face—
the same look I saw on men and young
Koori teenagers when I taught in
prison system, when I'd talk about
families, or love ...
faces turning red, and doing their best
to
hold back tears.
I've been drinking my arse off
here
trying to kill the blues
bouncing off the walls in my room.
I'm so far away, and so far out ...
trying to go out and do what I need to.
I'm still finding myself, just killing the blues.

Healing the Wounded

To attend to the wounds of invisibility,
it is essential that Aboriginal knowledge is promulgated,
and not only through the medium of Western academic discourse.
No. No.
My friend says:
we ought to tell our stories in our own words, Cuzo.
Our Dreaming stories …
is part of our culture and history …
use our own words, Joe
that way, it's all revealed—
trauma, joy—all the stuff that's usually left out
of them 'fischel writings.
Tellin' our stories, important man,
our ways.
Important for healing, Brother.
And, if healing's gonna happen,
we need a remembering,
not a forgetting
of our lives and things.

About Last Night

I dreamed last night
I played perfect guitar
singin'
Boulder to Birmingham.
I got this airplane just to fly,
then sad stories,
a last time.
I wrote my mother …
but Mother was gone.
I pretended the ocean took her
then, I rocked my soul …
the Bosom of Abraham.
Won't you sing me back.
Sing …
a dream.
Sing …
A scream
… an ice Creme.
Sing me too.

Full Moon Dreaming On Kamilaroi Country

Have been thinking about you this week
while on the road.
I know you've got dust on your shoes, too.

Couple of times, I thought I caught your face
on the face of slip streamers
as they flew by,
just a flash,
not a good long look …
but there was something there
as their car flew past,
that looked like you …

I love this song
and the soft, deep acoustic arrangement
is as beautiful
as the plains and the sky

and I thought I caught a glimpse of you
in the colours that flew away.
Into the bush of colours.
And we drove from
Country to Country,
carrying hearts.

And road kills lay silent, everywhere.
And I cried when
no one was looking.
And I'd choke to
hold back the tears.

I stood on the mountain
on Wayne's Country.
And wished I could jump off
and fly.
I thought I could see your face.

Carrying Hearts

The wattle's finished for the season.
The gums are grey.
The road ahead is black night.
We ride.
We're carrying hearts from Ngunnawal Country into Wiradjuri land.
We swerve the curves, and round the bends.
Rolling hills stretch to the horizon, surrounding us.

THREE

Shady

Sun-up comes slow on Sundays, in Shady. Willy wagtails go, 'chic-a, chic-a, chic-a' and, crows go, 'caw, caw, caoooooow'. And, the red-tail cockatoos, well, they just go bloody mad. The birds are always up early, doing their 'thing'—sneakin' up on worms, chewin' on stuff.

We're already showering and scrubbing ourselves stupid for Jesus, (again), (groan)! Never misses Church, my family. Oh no! Never. 'Onward, you Christian soldiers!' my stupid mother screeches at us if we're running late. 'Late for what?' Jesus will still be there, bleedin' all over the place. As usual. Dad's already in the driver's seat, waiting, playing Aboriginal music on the radio. He doesn't say much about Jesus. That's the one thing I really like about him. He's always goin' on 'bout Aboriginal 'stuff'—politics and legends tho, that's his go. And my stupid sister, Juri, (s'pose ta be short for Wiradjuri)—(Judge Juri, I call her. She hates it when I call her that, too. So, that's good 'nuff for me), well, she's dad's pet. She looks like him too: auburn-sunburn skin, brown hair, darker than me. My hair is gold … gold, like mum's. And I'm gonna keep it that way too!

Everyone's packed inside the bloody noisy volsie like sardines, and it's off to be saved again—from the devil.

'Morning Harry.'
'Morning, Father.'
'Morning family.'
'Good morning, Father.'

Stupid friggin' priest. He knows our names. Why doesn't he call us by 'em? Repressed wanka.

Take your seat. I'm on the end, always ready for the great escape. I do like the smell of the incense tho. Yeah, it's cool. They reckon that it was originally used to kill the stinkin' smell of the parishioners, or something. Here in Shady tho, it's used to mask the the stinkin' boozy breath of the stinkin' priest, Father Goode. Father No-good, I reckon.

The choir, in their red and whites look oh so innocent. I could tell ya a few stories about some of them! That's for sure! There are no bloody angels among that crew. And their Jesus knows it, too. The priests in their gold embroider robes, glide down the cold marble floor next, behind the choir and behind the Cross. The old Saints look down from their glassy panes—sword in hand, ready to smite the devil in us. They scare me, them bastards. They look so, angry. Did they ever smile? Laugh? I wonder?

'God be with you.'

'And also with you.'

'Please be seated ...'

Here we go again. Another lesson in the familiar. All repeated from last week. I wanna play with my phone, see who's on Facie. Better not pull it out tho, mum's got those 'Jesus eyes' on today, sees everything. Just hurry up, will ya, priest? Hymn. Prayer. Hymn. Another story about Him. Haven't these priests heard of Rest in Peace? They drag Him up every bloody week ... tell more lies about the poor man. Nail him up, again. More blood. Yuk. C'mon git to the wine, Father.

Finally, line-up for the sacrament. Kneel, tap out the Southern Cross on the body, hands up. 'Body of Christ'. (C'mon, where's the wine?) 'Blood of Christ'. I pretend I'm half blind and have to 'reach' for the goblet; just to tip it up a bit farther than Father would like to allow. From the taste of it, I'd say; 'Chateau Cheap Crap'.

Return to seats.

'Let us pray ...'

Eulogy. Prayer. Hymn. Prayer. Blessing. Ah-bloody men. Hymn as we leave.

'Thank you, Father.'

'Thank you, Harry.'

'Thank you, Father,' Juri and mum say in Christian harmony. I'm already at the old Volkswagen, can't wait to get home, get outa these church clothes.

'Outta here. Later, dudes.'

Finally! Finally, me and me Blundstone's are hittin' BlueSky Street. Don't step on a crack, less you break Jesus's back ... Oops! Sorry Jesus. Sorry Lord. I'll see ya next week. We'll make-up again then.

The Belonging Man

'This is difficult to say, but I'm for an art that is sentimental. My business is to make people cry.'—Christian Boltanski

'I know you've seen me walking in the rain.'

I slip the rain into a café bar with a million tables. I see you, way over there, beside the window—on the bright side, where the light shines strong.

I hang back here, on the shadow side, looking like I was born to this Shadow Bar, like I'm a be-longin' man.

And, there are much more than a million tables that separate you shiny folk from me.

Still, I watch you. Feel dirty. Lookin'. Seems wrong, somehow. But all I'm doing is comparing the worlds. Trying to understand it, that's all. Man!

Getting late, I can tell, even though there's no sun that can be seen from its place behind the clouds. Time's marked today all in the gloom —in the number of empty glasses ... all in the drunk memories.

Soon the afternoon crowd will push in and shoo barflies like me away—way back to the background. They'll fill their fill, laugh loud and take over. Us slow old boys, sneer from behind our cigarette stains and curly whiskers. We raise eyebrows at each other and (begrudgingly), shuffle away.

Later at the Blue Bar:

I touch your arm, feeling like there's no time to waste I look deep into your eyes. You stand rock steady, then slowly smile. Slowly. Lettin' me look into the shadow place, where you keep your memories. Back there, where the secrets lie. Openin' yourself ... you brush my arm, and you feel so good.

I see your Mob comin' to take you from me. Again.

I sneak in a fast line. 'Fuck it, C'mon. Let's blow this place wide—don't pay, jest run. That'll git 'em talkin'.'

A little giggle, you give me, but your eyes say, 'Not *now*! Later. We can … Soon.'

My eyes are filled with defeat. So, I drop it and play the 'good-sort'.

Yet still, you move to me—'Closer. Come and kiss.' I whisper. But, too late, they're here.

I stand shaking on weak legs, still thinking of tongue kissin' you, wondering if they can see the want on my mouth.

But eyes have wants too—I turn away to hide my look.

Your Mob are all smiles. Shake my hand. Doing their thang. Doing the right thing. I'm still thinking of that wild thing. You're thinking that way too. You catch my eye with a cheater's smile. Everyone knows that one, sweetheart. Your parent's caught you—they all seen you. And soon the news'll be out. They'll all know about us.

I hear your laugh as you walk off, pretending, playing innocent. You don't look back at me. I stand there, for a moment, messed up. Emptier than my glass.

I hold up your glass and close my eyes, smelling your lipstick stain on the rim. I'm still thinking of a kiss that could have been. It's only then I know how one person can be the whole room.

And how empty the room becomes after she's gone.

The Empty One:

Our giggles were free. Our touches, perfect. It was so wonderful, this loving. Lying with each other and lying to ourselves. Laying there, lying. That's all we were doing.

It's so wrong.

Funny thing, we didn't even like each other that much. We'd become more of a convenience. I didn't love her. She doesn't love me. But it's a way to escape the real, for a while. It's a way to get something we were missing—a way to be together. But it's so wrong and, we both knew it.

Didn't hear the door open. Didn't see the horror on his face when he found us. Didn't see him cry in his car in their driveway. Didn't watch him drink himself to sleep. I wasn't there to witness the end of their marriage or see the letter in the post citing 'Irreconcilable Differences'. But I heard the door slam.

Bang.

I imagined his heart break as I heard his footsteps grow weaker.

The room became cold when he slammed it shut on us. Our hot breaths turned icy as we turned on ourselves.

No words were spoken between us; we just sucked in breaths of shock, and panted cold air of failings from our open mouths. Disappointed desperation dripping off us.

Her eyes filled with tears.

Mine with worry.

'Oh God!' I prayed. 'No!'

I dressed first, and let myself out, saying nothing. Leaving her there, filled with fear.

Filling the Empty One with emptiness.

They Came Together

With Amelia Walker

They came together
From all over the place with dust on their boots,
books and a ravelling face.
Poets, Academics, Keepers of Stories
stars bright and eyes still shining.
I watch, listen, watch
try to remember names ...
You're here, but, in me every second, you walk in me,
over me, beside and behind, like the puppet in the light on the canvas.
I love it all ...
the glad, sad the long, short and tall words
which opens a new space, a beginning,
that's smoking hot.

                              Together, we came
                         in boots dusted with all over,
                     our faces like books, coming unbound
                    with stories, unke(m)pt academics—poets
              and 'I's finding silence among daylight stars eclipsed:
                              listen, watch, listen
                          ... names—remember—try
                      be here, in every second, walking and still
                  as a canvas, alive with shadows, puppeting their dances.
                                 All of it, I love.
                      Words grow tall, short, long, sad, glad,
                          beginning space anew, opening
                              —a real cool blaze.

Spooky!

Wanna hear a ghost story?

On Easter Monday, I had to record a lecture for a class I am teaching. I do not have Internet access at my home. When I require internet, I usually go to a place named To All My Friends, just down the road from where I live.

Only that, To All My Friends does not open on Mondays!

So, on this Easter Monday I went to the university, to my office. I needed to do a fair piece of research reading on the topic before I could record the lecture, on-line.

The research took me about four hours, I am a very slow reader, and the topic is in a subject area that I had not taught before. By the time I was prepared to record the lecture, the sun was casting long shadows over the building.

My office is the last office, down a long corridor. My desk faces a window, through which I see people coming and going from Uni. There are gum trees and long grass near my office on campus, and often a family of grey kangaroos can be seen feeding in the late afternoon.

Building 20, (my office block), is an old building, made from brick, stands tired and worn. It is one of the original buildings of the university built thirty years ago. Building 20 has seen many, many students and teachers and administrative staff come and leave, through the years. The elevator is a creaky old job that on more than one occasion in the past five years has had motor failings, trapping a staff member until a technician was able to release them from within. The long corridors have an element of aloneness and a kind of sadness about them, I've noticed.

On Monday, I was the only person on my floor. I had worked many years in this building, I wrote my PhD in an office three doors down from the office I work in now. I feel I know this old place well.

On occasions though, I have thought that there is an 'un-earthly' presence on the floor where I work, but I mostly dismiss the 'feeling' as just my wild imagination running away with me.

I seem to remember that the great physicist, Einstein, wrote of 'ghost spirits' that appear as apparitions to people, as being the 'spirits' of people who have died, whose energy force—(the spirit), had collided from the universe in which they are in, with the universe in which we (live people) are in. Einstein said that the ghost has possibly made an accident in that collision of the two universes and has 'slipped' into our universe and here it remains, trapped, trying to find its way back to beyond.

Hmm!

I began recording the lecture on my computer.

My office is always wide open as I do not like being inside closed rooms. From the corner of my eye, I can see the hallway through the office door. The lecture I was recording took me an hour, at which time the sun was gone beyond the horizon. It had become very dark outside.

As I was recording, I thought I could see a 'movement', or a flash of 'black something' at my doorway. I looked to see who was there … there was no one there. I checked the corridor, only to find it empty of people. I called, 'Anyone there?'

I waited for any reply, but no reply was forthcoming.

This thing happened again a few minutes later. I looked again to find no one there.

These phenomena continued through the hour of my recording.

As I completed the recording, I sat back deep into my chair and drew a long breath. It had been a long afternoon of work, and I suddenly felt tired. I closed my eyes and rested for a minute. During my little rest, I thought I felt a light tug on my shirt sleeve. I opened my eyes and turned to see if I had in fact caught my shirt on a part of the chair. It had not. I ran my fingers through my hair, closing my eyes, when I felt the tug on my sleeve again. I wasn't imagining the pull on my shirt the second time.

'Ghost,' I thought.

I began to gather my books and keys and packed my bag with these things, and retrieved my mobile phone from the charging socket, when a book fell from the bookshelf directly behind me.

I turned quickly to see what, if anything, had caused the book to fall. I could not see anything, person or ghost, that might have caused the book to fall. I turned back to collect my bag when a second book fell from the bookshelf.

'Okay! I'm going.' I spoke aloud to thin air.

I left the office, closing the door behind me when I heard a third book hit the floor in there.

I left the building in the dark early night and hurried to my car which had been parked about one hundred meters away. The feeling of being followed by something or someone I could not see, washed over me, the entire distance to the car.

Once inside my car, the feeling of being watched, or pursued, stopped.

I was glad to drive home, a little shaken, and a bit the worse for wear and tear.

The next day I returned to my office to find the three books from the bookshelf, a top each other, directly behind the chair I had been sitting in the day before.

Spooky!

re[her]sal

art, pretender
finger every pie,
you lie, and re[live]ed, again,
you big miss, me
shot on the Up. passive/aggressive
hater and love, big miss
all the death, blown bits
talk horse and talk art
you freak.
Great re[her]sal, crowd surfer, big miss
me you die, liar, live
again, after the gReat One, reigned
and then
the big nUmber 2
who lose? you live to serve the mass
you're a-gas
re[live]ed … re[hearse]Al, moody man
colour kids, draw white lines, drawn
upon the dirt wall
where's the rock, there's crumble
outside the gas
inside re[hearse]
it all
never ends …

Some Popular Australian Mistakes (22 Thoughts on a Dead Bullock)

With Jen Crawford

22. The blackfellow is a fraud. A white man can learn to throw the boomerang as well as an aborigine—even better. A blackfellow is not to be depended on with regard to direction, distance or weather. A blackfellow once offered to take us to better water than that at which we were camping. He said it was only half-a-mile. We rolled up our swags and followed him and his gin five miles through the scrub to a mud-hole with a dead bullock in it. Also, he said that it would rain that night; and it didn't rain there for six months. Moreover, he threw a boomerang at a rabbit and lamed one of his dogs—of which he had about 150.

—Henry Lawson, 'SOME POPULAR AUSTRALIAN MISTAKES,' published in the *Bulletin*, 18 November 1893.

1. Maybe Lawson needed water or maybe he needed a long walk. Maybe he needed a good hard look at a dead bullock's eye.

2. Who's looking for the pattern of prints around the waterhole—looking for brolga prints, pelican prints, roo prints, emu prints, euro prints, bustard prints, lizard prints? Who's got those patterns? Who's got those names?

3. Who's got the patterns of rabbit paws, fox paws, horse hooves, camel hooves, donkey hooves, sheep hooves, cow hooves, bullock hooves, bullock hooves, bullock hooves, bullock hooves?

4. Some creatures drink and drink and drink, and never stop being thirsty.

5. A Barkindji man drew the patterns on his dry skin …

6. White doctors took that Barkindji man's lung, and left a jagged pattern upon the black man's body.

7. Barkindji named that river, Barka.

8. White men re-named that river Darling, in honour of Sir John.

9. Once I saw a dead sheep with its stomach leather split. In the sack of the stomach was bright green grass, like mulch in the catcher of the mower.

10. Who's sweeping scum from the surface of the water? Scooping out mud. Teasing out plants that clog up the flow.

11. You can't drink what's got dung in it. You can't drink what's got a dead animal in it. You can't drink what's already drunk. You can't drink from a vessel that's cracked. Not for long, anyway.

12. If you put up a fence, the plants come back. Water can be clean flowing. But where are you going to put the fence?

13. You can't breathe air through the mud on the banks if the bank's been trampled hard.

14. You can trace the lines of fish in the Barwon. Tracing the prints back from the flow to the source.

15. Margaret said that Mooda-gatta was there that day, at the place by the river, rushing her on the bank, sending up a waterspout.

16. Nyemba people say the Mooda-gatta is a water-dog, but it's not a canine.

17. Rainbow Serpent made that waterway. She is law.

18. Whitemen took away the clean water for themselves, left muddy paste for the fish and the Black people.

19. Gertie told us stories of the country, of hard days and nights of droving, of labour, of the birthing tree.

20. Bradley keeps the river stories now, near the ochre pit, shared by four clans. At the museum he speaks wise.

21. Wayne keeps the stories of the land in his head, not writing them down to be taken away.

22. Dhigarrbila still digs. Ngurri stills looks out over the grasslands. Bandarr boxes on. Guugaarr is still the giant in the grass. Kultarr leaves tiny prints on the sand.

I See You

With Alice Bishop

Give your power away. Here.
Lose control.
More interesting the more I ponder it,
but I didn't like it at first.

I wanna know more about these animals,
I can tell u something about crow.

What's that sound?
Black lightning?
Bang, bang …
Barkindji feet did not have time to stand, to fight, nor run
the day the fires burned out. (can feel the pounding beat)

Anyway, you say, Paul,

Those politicians. On the news.
Talk.
COVID, Alice.
They say it's spreading … like bushfire.
Have you heard about those birds that use fire? The whistling kite?
Fire's not all bad.
Not a bad thing before.
We used it for good.
We use it for good.

(That softness, inside of a wrist.
Those yellow-crested birds can live to 80. How many fires have those birds
seen before?

A lot of people in this country are lucky to live to 60, not 80. Stop writing about birds.
Stop writing about bushfire).

Do you run with Will-Du, big spirit dog, on night skies?
Do you whine your name on wind, through the age?
Have I met you on a cemented park?

Broken by wind and rain, the bones of my people speak. What else broke them?
And, in the North country, the land is fire dancing—Burning, burning life and limb.
(ouch! too good)
(Farther away, no eyes turned to watch).
My love coughed her last breath ...
I have nothing to bury
my arms fall right through—
leaving me grasping dust.
They're held in the grip of trees and with silent spirits,
They turn blanks into banks of sound.
But what is sound anyway?
Beautiful work.

Tomorrow

With Bethaney Turner

The tomorrow
came
in ways already
known to harm
too familiar
too demanding
first begging, then insisting
to be other
what had they learned from their fathers?
what could Country teach them?
Nothing
without heart and broken hands.

Reconcile That

With Jen Crawford

'Few of those who have experienced the crocodile's death roll have lived to describe it. It is, essentially, an experience beyond words of total terror'.
—Val Plumwood

1

unsure / kind of
        the history feels a bit shoved down our throats
                we were never taught any of this stuff
bit nervous
          I expected there would be less about the past and so
          forth
        I'm not sure what the identity stuff has to do with this subject
I'm not sure what culture has to do with the subject
I'm once again aware of the enormous hole in my education
                              I just want the information
       I just want to know how to write
                     I'm not sure what to write
       I don't know where to start

Buried truths and spoken lies have become the national ID,
you just can't make heroes from slaughter and theft.
But Mother Earth won't easily rest with buried lies.
Mother Earth gives up her dead, and the bones must be explained.
        Nhantama. Nhantama—
—again, again, She gives up her dead ...
there are just too many bones.
This is hard to swallow ...
We First Nations peoples have truths kulpa—(to tell, to talk).

Can you listen, papu?
Can you Australians listen for truth to come out?
This isn't sweet cake.
This is bitter tea.

Australians, we want you to thalti—(to listen, to hear)
Hear First Nations creation stories.
Hear the destruction stories too.
Don't talk loud at us. Don't drown our voice this time with Commissions and variations.

Thalti—We want you to listen and to hear.

I know where it started
I know when, too …
Word came fast to us, on the wind … even Waku and Bilyara didn't fly that day. Hmmm,
then we saw the smoke …
                        Barkindji.

2

he reassured me that it's okay to not instantly understand
        I love Canberra, it's where I grew up
When I used to think of nature I would only think of the pretty things
        now, I know what it cost the Ngunnawal people
I had walked past these things nearly every day and never once stopped & digested why they are there …
        I slowly realised my respect for different creatures around me
        I still love Canberra, but it seems different to me now

Through My Window

If you only see heat waves on an endless nothing,
and if you hate it, then close your eyes.
Don't poison yourself with the strain.
If you are sickened by the smell of saltbush on kangaroo,
block your nostrils; fill your nose instead
with your own familiar smells.
If it's only sticky heat you feel upon your skin out there,
and you hate it ... wash yourself out.
Don't wear it.
You won't see what I know when I see through my window ...
Nor will you smell the Country on every breath as sweet bush honey.
Brown snakes cover my home; black birds fill the sky ...
I don't block out the sun when sweat is on my body— I keep it all.
Spring is the song on every Bee's buzz through my window,
—the smell of honey, drifting on wind from Black Wattle
in bloom is as beautiful as you ...

Through Your Window

With K A Nelson

Eyes open, wanting to see how and what you see,
but it is not my country.
You took me there, showed me black snakes, black birds,
encouraged me to smell bush honey, listen to bees, talk
to wind, but I don't speak its Tongue. Like you,
I sweated in sun, but ran to shade.
I wanted to bathe every second day,
but
I walked with you, looked through your window.

Through Our Window

With Rina Kikuchi

Do I see what you see?
Do I see what's behind what you see?
It's your country I am standing
Water surging calmly reflecting the skies on surface
I hear the frogs sing
I smell more rain coming
The taste of saltbush tingles the tip of my tongue
The frilled lizard you pointed gradually shaped its outline
for me
It took a while
but I see it now
I don't read the stars filling the dark sky
but I wonder if I ever will
I may never see what you see
but we stand side by side
looking at the river, My Darling, My Love,

listening to the stories of the Land

Tomorrow Tonight

Its Australia Day, tomorrow.
And
I'm Drinkin'.
Alone tonight.
And Australians are looking at me funny,
looking back, after they pass me.

I'd rise to meet the challenge
with vigour in the past.
And do the business.
And break my hands.
And sometimes, I'd break my heart on targets.

Now, it's different to me.
They are too stupid. These Australians.
And I used to be too wild, anyway.
Tomorrow they will wave flags
Toot horns
think they are Kings.
I'll do the museum.
Recite poetry
And claim Country …
as it Always was
and Always will be …

Sometimes

I dont think beyond my wild head
And my head rings with
Rage.
And in blind light
I don't see
you
Or me
Or anything.
Its just dark
and,
I'm 's'posed to understand.
News is out
All over town
'bout me.
Leave now
No winner here.
Not again.
Don't trust in you
and you Don't trust in me
Words don't mean a thing.
Everyone knows.
Nothing can be done
if You win again.

(Thanks Hank)

Guys Like Me They Don't Want

Used to meet a guy
down on Basin Street
opposite the Park …
he spoke with a French accent
said he was from New Orleans.
Yeah, I questioned.
Oui, he said.
He smiled a liar's grin …
He sold good Gas.
She'd blow your head …
how come you're here then?
I looked hard.
Brother smiled.
They're trying to do away
with guys like me

I felt so needin', that lovin',
I fell down, Oh Paul …
wanted so to be loved.
No one's around.
No one love me at all.
So how come you're here then, I asked myself? …
I thought, Brother,
they're trying to put an end
to guys like me.

Doctor. Oh Doctor.
What's wrong with 'Tre-ees
she's blowin'. Wrong way

Leaves are leavin' her too.
How come she's still here then …
cause they're trying
to put an end to guys
like her, too.

Acknowledgments

I would like to thank my colleagues at the University of Canberra, particularly Jen Crawford for her great friendship and guidance in writing and in poetry and for her sharing of poems and poetry with me over the past nine years, whom without that sharing, I would not be where I am today with writing.

I would also like to thank Paul Magee for his support.

I am grateful to Jen Crawford, Amelia Walker, Alice Bishop, Bethaney Turner, K A Nelson and Rina Kikuchi for being open to collaborating on poems in this collection and agreeing to publish them here.

Thanks to Shane Strange at Recent Work Press for publishing this collection and particularly to K A Nelson who collated and edited this manuscript into its current form.

'Wita Witalana (look out over)' was commissioned by *Kindred Trees*, in 2021. The project encourages love of trees through poetry in association with ACT Tree register. See: kindredtrees.com.au

'Some popular Australian Mistakes' first appeared in *Rabbit: A Journal for Nonfiction Poetry*.

'Women's Country' first appeared in *Difficult Conversations*.

'About Last Night' and 'So Deep the Blue' first appeared in *Westerly Magazine*.

'Reconcile That', 'Brown Snake Night…Sing to Me Too' and 'Strangers in that Country' first appeared in *Axon: Creative Explorations*.

About the Author

Paul Collis is a Barkindji man. He was born in Bourke, in far north/west New South Wales. His early life was informed by Barkindji and Kunya and Murawarri, and Wongamara and Nyempa story tellers and artists, who taught him Aboriginal Culture and Law. Paul earned his Doctorate at University Canberra in 2015, for a study of Barkindji identity with a specific focus on masculinity. His first novel, *Dancing Home* won the 2017 *David Unaipon Award*, and the 2019 ACT Book of the year Award. Paul's first poetry collection, *Nightmares Run Like Mercury*, was published by Recent Work Press in 2021. Paul works as Director, Indigenous Engagement, in the Faculty of Arts and Design at the University of Canberra.

www.ingramcontent.com/pod-product-compliance
Lightning Source LLC
Chambersburg PA
CBHW060619080526
44585CB00013B/895